OUR
NATIONAL
DISGRACE

OUR
NATIONAL
DISGRACE

HOMELESSNESS IN THE CITY OF ANGELS

The *Los Angeles Times* Editorial Board

INTRODUCTION BY NICHOLAS GOLDBERG

Heyday, Berkeley, California

Library of Congress Cataloging-in-Publication Data
is available.

Book and cover design by Ashley Ingram
Cover photo and all interior photos by Francine Orr/
  Los Angeles Times

Printed in East Peoria, Illinois, by Versa Press, Inc.

10 9 8 7 6 5 4 3 2 1

CONTENTS

INTRODUCTION

With the gap between rich and poor continuing to widen in the United States, with housing prices rising at double the rate of wages, and with nearly half the country convinced that government aid to the needy does more harm than good, it should perhaps come as no surprise that homelessness remains at crisis levels in cities around the nation.

According to the latest figures from the US Department of Housing and Urban Development, there are now more than 550,000 people in the country who lack a "fixed, regular, and adequate" place to sleep on any given night.

To highlight the continuing reality of homelessness and destitution in one of the world's richest countries, a special UN-appointed monitor on "extreme poverty" recently undertook an unusual fact-finding mission around the United States. At the end of his two-week mission through Alabama, California, West Virginia, and Washington DC, among other places, he criticized the United States for rejecting access to housing and sanitation as essential human rights and spoke scathingly of America's "bid to become the most unequal society in the world."

The good news is that homelessness has been steadily declining around the country since 2006. But California has defied that trend. It is here—where 25 percent of all the nation's homeless people live—that the problem is concentrated, and it is in Los Angeles where the problem is most severe and most visible. Here, homelessness is not hidden in emergency shelters as it is in New York. Tent cities and sprawling squatter camps have spread from downtown

LA's dismal and notorious Skid Row to the farthest reaches of Los Angeles County. Destitution is visible on a daily basis—men, women, and children sleeping in alleyways, begging in shopping centers, keeping dry in tunnels, underpasses, and train stations. The extent and severity of Los Angeles's homelessness problem has set up an inevitable tension between the needs of the city and the rights of the homeless, and, as in other cities, has provoked an unavoidable fight over what are the best solutions and who should make the sacrifices to achieve them.

Of course, neither the fact of homelessness nor the debate over how to address it is new to this city. Nor is the temptation to blame the victims themselves.

As early as 1882, in its second year of publication, the *Los Angeles Times* wrote that the city was "infested with vagrants...an insolent, impudent and vicious lot." The editorial continued: "Don't feed the worthless chaps. It only encourages them in their idleness and viciousness.

There is no cause for begging. They could all get work at good wages if they would accept it. Whenever a healthy vag solicits a meal or money you do not do your duty if you do not inform the police and have the beggar arrested."

A year later, the city passed an ordinance promi-sing fines and punishments to anyone who didn't seek employment, who solicited alms, who roamed from place to place, was idle or dissolute or lewd or lived in a "house of ill fame," or was a common prostitute or drunkard or vagrant.

Homelessness in Los Angeles spiked during the Great Depression. (That's when *The Times* praised the chief of the Los Angeles Police Department for turning back tramps and hobos at the state's borders "regardless of opinion as to the strict legality of [his] measures.") And homelessness became a national issue again after the deinstitutionalization of mental asylums. The *Los Angeles Times* won a Pulitzer Prize in 2002 for a series of editorials on the civil liberties of mentally ill people living on the streets.

Today, with an acute housing shortage in California and increasing gentrification leading to displacement in Los Angeles, the numbers are climbing again. Homelessness has risen every year in LA since 2013.

It was against this dismal backdrop that the *Los Angeles Times* editorial board set out to address the homelessness catastrophe, raise awareness, clear up misconceptions, exhort politicians to action—and then try to sort out the paths forward. Our six-part series began at the end of February 2018.

The editorials raised a number of fundamental questions about homelessness: Is it an indicator of a fatal flaw in our market economies? Is it an inevitable by-product of our selfish insistence on a single-family-home lifestyle? Is it the result of the decision by liberal civil libertarians—or, conversely, Ronald Reagan—to close the nation's mental institutions? Is it the Democrats' fault? The Republicans'? Is it driven by mental illness and drug addiction or by poverty?

We took on a variety of complicated policy issues that face not just Los Angeles but cities around the country, including the inevitable battle over the siting of homeless housing in residential neighborhoods, the need to balance the rights of the homeless with the rights of other city residents, and the continuing efforts to bring services to the mentally ill homeless. A staff photographer and a videographer illustrated the series with shocking images of people living on the streets all across the city—images that would be even more shocking if they weren't so increasingly familiar.

For decades, politicians have promised solutions to the problem of homelessness, but have fallen short. In Los Angeles, as elsewhere, this has been due to fractious, competitive local politics and fear on the part of elected officials of a powerful voter backlash against the kinds of solutions that are required to address the problem.

But in fact, Los Angeles voters have made it clear at the ballot box in recent years that they are ready for strong action to address the problem—and that they're willing to pay billions of dollars in new taxes to ensure that housing gets built for the homeless and that social services are provided for those who need them. We hope that this editorial series will help persuade those with the power to make change that waiting for the problem to go away—or, more likely, to get worse—is no solution at all.

I

LOS ANGELES'S HOMELESSNESS CRISIS IS A NATIONAL DISGRACE

A man sits quietly on a sidewalk in the Skid Row
neighborhood of Los Angeles.

THERE ARE FEW SIGHTS IN THE WORLD LIKE NIGHTTIME in Skid Row, the teeming Dickensian dystopia in downtown Los Angeles where homeless and destitute people have been concentrated for more than a century.

Here, men and women sleep in rows, lined up one after another for block after block in makeshift tents or on cardboard mats on the sidewalks—the mad, the afflicted, and the disabled alongside those who are merely down on their luck. Criminals prey on them, drugs such as heroin and crystal meth are easily available, sexual assault and physical violence are common, and infectious diseases like tuberculosis, hepatitis, and AIDS are constant threats.

Skid Row is—and long has been—a national disgrace, a grim reminder of man's ability to turn his back on his fellow man. But these days it is only the ugly epicenter of a staggering homelessness problem that radiates outward for more than 100 miles throughout Los Angeles County and beyond. There are now more than fifty-seven thousand people who lack a "fixed, regular, or adequate place to sleep" on any given night in the county, and fewer than 1 in 10 of them are in Skid Row.

Homelessness burst its traditional borders several years ago, spreading first to gloomy underpasses and dim side streets, and then to public parks and library reading rooms and subway platforms. No matter where you live in LA County, from Long Beach to Beverly Hills to Lancaster, you cannot credibly claim today to be unaware of the squalid tent cities, the sprawling encampments, or the despair and misery on display there.

At last, the problem became so acute—and so visible—that Los Angeles took extraordinary action. To your credit, to all of our credit, the citizens of this city and this county voted in November 2016 and again in March 2017 to raise our own taxes to fund an enormous multi-billion-dollar, ten-year program of housing and social services for the homeless.

As a result, Los Angeles now has its best chance in decades to combat homelessness—an opportunity that surely all can agree must not be wasted. It is neither desirable nor morally acceptable nor practical for this city or this county to blithely tolerate the signs of destitution more commonly associated with 1980s Calcutta or the slums of Rio de Janiero or medieval Europe. We cannot go on shutting our windows to beggars at freeway offramps or stepping casually over men and women curled up in sleeping bags or turning away when people who have no access to public bathrooms use the city streets as toilets. We cannot indefinitely roust people who have nowhere to go or confiscate their belongings or criminalize their struggle for basic necessities. Such desperate stopgap measures are not solutions, but emblems of a deteriorating city, admissions of failure. We now have the opportunity to do better.

BUT HERE'S THE BAD NEWS: Passing Measures H and HHH was the easy part. Money alone doesn't solve problems, and in the end the tougher questions are how to spend it, where to spend it, on whom to spend it, and how to measure success. If we hope that the crisis will be gone—or, more realistically, under control—when the money runs out in 10 years, we need city and county officials to explain what actions they're taking and why, how many people they've housed or failed to house, what they expect to accomplish by the end of the year and by the end of the decade—so that we can hold them accountable for their actions.

Furthermore, those politicians who have for too long shamefully shirked their responsibility to address the festering problems must now exercise real leadership; they must stop pandering to the vocal minority of residents who object to housing for homeless and low-income people in their neighborhoods. Years of infighting, mixed messages, and failures of political will must come to an end.

All the region's politicians must step up, but especially Mayor Eric Garcetti—whose legacy and political future will rise or fall on how he handles this colossal urban crisis—and the members of the Los Angeles City Council, who have too often allowed political expediency and timidity to guide their actions. Homelessness in the city of Los Angeles has risen every year since Garcetti took office in 2013. Over the course of his tenure, it is up 49 percent.

County officials have made some progress—breaking down bureaucratic silos, leveraging new federal Medicaid dollars, setting sensible goals and priorities, using Measure H money to quadruple the number of homeless outreach teams, add shelter beds, and help with rental subsidies—but they too have an enormous task ahead of them. And homelessness, which does

"IN AMERICA, HOUSING IS
A COMMODITY. IF YOU CAN
AFFORD IT, YOU HAVE IT;
IF YOU CAN'T, YOU DON'T."

—GARY BLASI,
UCLA LAW PROFESSOR EMERITUS

not recognize municipal boundaries, is also present in most of the other eighty-seven cities in LA County, many of which have historically tried to push the poor and homeless out, hoping the problem would go away. Only three cities in the county are on track to meet their "fair share" housing construction goals.

How did we get here? From the founding of this newspaper in 1881, the pages of *The Times* have been filled with stories of those we have called, at various times, vagrants, hobos, tramps, transients, and drifters. And for as long as there have been homeless people, there has been a tendency to blame the victims themselves for their condition—to see their failure to thrive as an issue of character, of moral weakness, of laziness. Since the "deinstitutionalization" of the mentally ill in the second half of the twentieth century, and the subsequent failure of government to provide the promised outpatient services for those who had been released, the problem has grown significantly worse.

Today, a confluence of factors is driving people onto the streets. The shredding of the safety net in Washington and California is one. (Consider the inexcusable shortage of federal Section 8 vouchers for subsidized low-income housing, or the dismally low level of "general relief payments" for the county's neediest single adults.)

At the same time, California is experiencing a severe housing shortage. Gentrification is taking more and more once-affordable rental units off the LA market, and restrictive zoning laws along with high construction costs and anti-development sentiment make new affordable units hard to build. Over the last six years, the rent for a studio apartment here has climbed 92 percent, according to UCLA law professor emeritus Gary Blasi, so that even people who have jobs can find themselves living on the streets after a rent spike or an unexpected crisis. As Blasi notes, "In America, housing is a commodity. If you can afford it, you have it; if you can't, you don't."

CONTRARY TO POPULAR BELIEF, the homeless in Los Angeles are not mostly mentally ill or drug addicted, raving or matted-haired or frightening—although a sizable minority meet some of those descriptions. They are not mostly people who drifted in from other states in search of a comfy climate in which to sponge off of others; the overwhelming majority have lived in the region for years. Today, a greater and greater proportion of people living on the streets are there because of bad luck or a series of mistakes, or because the economy forgot them—they lost a job or were evicted or fled an abusive marriage just as the housing market was growing increasingly unforgiving.

It will surprise no one to learn that it is the most vulnerable among us who usually end up without a place to live. According to the Los Angeles Homeless Services Authority, more than five thousand of the county's nearly fifty-eight thousand homeless people are children and more than four thousand are elderly. About one-third are mentally ill. Some 40 percent are African American. Also heavily represented: Veterans. The disabled. Young people from the county's overwhelmed juvenile justice system and its foster care programs. Men and women released from jail, without the tools or skills needed for reentering society. Patients released from public hospitals—often with untreated cancers, infections, or diabetes. Victims of domestic violence.

All the great social issues of American society play out in homelessness—inequality, racial injustice, poverty, violence, sexism. Naturally, life expectancy for the homeless is short: about forty-seven years, according to Skid Row doctor Susan Partovi, compared with seventy-eight in the population as a whole.

Solutions to the problem vary, depending on which portion of the homeless population you're trying to help. In the months and years ahead, many more supportive housing units (which include access to social services and treatment) must be sited and built for the chronically homeless, as promised by Measure HHH—in all parts of the city, not just where the backlash will be weakest. To this end, city politicians (who have control over land-use policies) must lead rather than be led by a vocal minority of obstructionist constituents. At the same time, for the region's "economically homeless," the state's broader housing crisis must be addressed by new laws and incentives that encourage construction, especially of subsidized affordable housing. For the good of the city itself, short-term needs must be weighed against long-term solutions and officials must find the right balance between managing the homelessness problem and eradicating it. The rights of people living on the streets must be protected and balanced against the needs of the city.

The challenges are enormous, even if everyone is pulling in the same direction. That reality was driven home this month by a new Los Angeles Homeless Services Authority report showing that the county's homeless population is increasing faster than the supply of new housing, despite the millions of dollars already flowing in from the two ballot measures.

In one of the world's richest nations, homelessness on this scale should be shameful and shocking. But most Angelenos are no longer either shocked or shamed. Increasingly, we are uncomfortable, irritated, disgusted, scared, or oblivious. Compassion is being replaced by resignation.

Yet we all know the truth: The men curled up in the sleeping bags and the women pushing the overflowing shopping carts or talking to invisible interlocutors on the subways could, if the world were just a slightly different place, be our mothers, our brothers, our friends, ourselves.

It is imperative that we act now so that we don't wake up in five, ten, or twenty years wondering where we were or what we could possibly have been thinking or why we kept quiet and did nothing as this unconscionable catastrophe took hold.

II

THE HOMELESS ARE NOT
WHO YOU THINK THEY ARE

Nadia kisses her son Sebastian.

MANY PEOPLE THINK OF HOMELESSNESS AS A PROBLEM of substance abusers and mentally ill people, of chronic Skid Row street-dwellers pushing shopping carts. But increasingly, the crisis in Los Angeles today is about a less visible (but more numerous) group of "economically homeless" people. These are people who have been driven onto the streets or into shelters by hard times, bad luck, and California's irresponsible failure to address its own housing needs.

Consider Nadia, whose story has become typical. When she decided she had to end her abusive marriage, she knew it would be hard to find an affordable place to live with her three young children. With her husband, she had paid $2,000 a month for a three-bedroom condo in the San Fernando Valley, but prices were rising rapidly, and now two-bedroom apartments in the area were going for $2,400—an impossible rent for a single parent who worked part time at Magic Mountain.

For months she hunted while staying with family and friends. She qualified for a unit in a low-income housing project, but the waiting list was two years long. She obtained a federal Section 8 voucher to subsidize the rent in a market-rate apartment, but landlord after landlord refused to accept Section 8, or charged a rent that was too high to meet the federal government's unrealistically low "fair-market rent" limit.

Nadia and her rambunctious young kids eventually wore out their welcome at the houses where they were staying. They found themselves left with little choice, with neither a place of their own nor a friend to fall back on. Last summer, they took refuge at San Fernando Valley Rescue Mission's shelter for homeless families.

NADIA AND HER CHILDREN are among the economically homeless—men, women, and, often enough, families, who find themselves without a place to live because of some kind of setback or immediate crisis: a divorce, a short-term illness, a loss of a job, an eviction. In many cities across the nation, these are not necessarily problems that would plunge a person into homelessness. But here they can. Why? Because of the shockingly high cost of housing in Los Angeles.

For decades, Southern California—stuck in a low-density, single-family, not-in-my-backyard twentieth-century mindset—has failed to build enough housing to keep up with population growth and demand. Rents are at an all-time high. Stagnant incomes and a shortage of middle-class jobs mean more people are struggling. The safety net hasn't grown to catch all the people in need, nor has public sympathy always been on their side. In 2006, LA city voters rejected a $1 billion bond to create ten thousand residential units for low-income and homeless people, thus exacerbating the housing shortage.

Today, we are paying the price: The economically homeless are now estimated to make up more than half of LA's unhoused—and it is their rising numbers that are fueling the unprecedented growth in that population. More than half of the people surveyed by the Los Angeles Homeless Services Authority last year said they were homeless because of an eviction, foreclosure, unemployment, or "financial reasons."

In just six years, the median rent for a one-bedroom apartment in Los Angeles County has increased 67 percent, from about $1,200 to $2,000, according to Zillow's Rent Index. The median household income during the same period increased only 23 percent, from $52,280 in 2011 to $64,300 in 2017.

Today, one in three renters in the Los Angeles metropolitan area is considered "severely rent burdened," meaning they spend at least half their income on housing. Los Angeles County is the most unaffordable region in the country for the poorest renters, according to the US Department of Housing and Urban Department. To understand just how thin the line is between those with a place to live and those without, consider a study conducted by Zillow estimating that a rent increase of 5 percent in Los Angeles County would push two thousand people into homelessness.

Guadalupe Linares is an example of someone who teeters on the edge. She and her two children moved out of a $600-a-month illegally converted garage after a rat bit her son. But the one-bedroom she found cost twice as much, forcing her to take on long hours in multiple jobs, including cleaning houses and working in restaurants. Her seventeen-year-old daughter, Mariana, who had been thinking about a career in medicine, began missing school to help her mom clean houses from seven in the morning to eleven at night—which required her to transfer to an independent study program through the school district. She quickly learned that the program is full of kids putting their ambitions on hold while they work to help keep their families housed.

This cannot be Los Angeles's future.

To end the housing shortage that is driving rents to unaffordable levels, Los Angeles County and its cities have to allow construction. A lot of it. We're not talking, in this instance, about permanent supportive housing for chronically homeless people—that sort of housing (which includes access to social services and substance abuse and mental health treatment) is absolutely essential and is being built under Measure HHH in Los Angeles. The economically homeless need something else: affordable housing that offers below-market rents for low-income people. And regular market-rate housing as well that will increase the supply and help bring down rents for everyone.

Since 1980, far fewer homes have been built than are needed to meet population growth in the county, according to the Southern California

A CITY CANNOT SAY IT'S FULL. THE REGION MUST BUILD DENSER AND TALLER TO MAKE SPACE FOR THE PEOPLE WHO ARE ALREADY HERE.

Association of Governments, and now the county has a deficit of nearly one million housing units. The vast majority of the eighty-eight cities in the county are not adding enough market-rate and affordable housing to meet their fair share of the region's growth.

Sure, there are some legitimate excuses—land costs are high and environmental concerns have slowed development. But far too often, residents and elected officials act on their worst NIMBY instincts to block or restrict housing in the name of preventing traffic and density and protecting neighborhood character. One Torrance city councilman argued against building new homes, saying, "A city should be allowed to say we're full."

No—a city cannot say it's full. Too many people are clinging to an old vision of Southern California, when orange groves were plowed under for single-family subdivisions, wide avenues, and freeways. Today, those ranch homes cost $1 million and more, the roads are clogged, and working-class families can end up living in their cars. The region must build denser and taller to make space for the people who are already here. That doesn't require Dubai-style skyscrapers; it can mean more townhomes and four-story apartment buildings and high-rises near transit.

The state passed new laws last year to pressure cities to accommodate more housing and to streamline approvals in communities that have failed to keep up with population growth. California lawmakers also approved new funding for affordable housing and gave cities the authority to enact inclusionary zoning laws, which require that affordable units be built in market-rate housing developments. These are positive steps, but the state should adopt even more aggressive mandates if cities continue to throw up hurdles. In some cases, this will change the look, feel, and character of cities. But that's an inevitable result of population growth.

OF COURSE, IT WILL TAKE YEARS to catch up on housing construction. In the meantime, rent hikes and evictions will continue. That's why policymakers must make the prevention of homelessness a cornerstone of their efforts. To that end, Los Angeles County plans to use Measure H funds to provide temporary rental assistance to help people on the brink of losing an apartment. It's easier and cheaper to keep people in housing than to help them off the street after the fact.

The county is also funding legal services to help poor renters fight eviction or to help them qualify for relocation assistance. Fewer than 1 percent of renters facing eviction have lawyers. Cities should also consider passing laws to require that landlords show "just cause" to evict.

The federal government has not done enough. HUD should significantly increase funding for the Section 8 voucher program in Los Angeles County, taking into account the high cost of housing here. Section 8 rental vouchers are pegged to HUD's "fair-market rents," which are often substantially less than actual market rents.

Ultimately, there has to be a recognition that every new apartment unit rejected is a family denied an affordable place to live. Just as Los Angeles voters were willing to say yes to higher taxes for homeless housing and services, they have to be willing to say yes to the housing construction in their neighborhoods. That will, over time, alleviate the shortage.

Nadia notes that it is not laziness or drinking or drug abuse that's plunging so many people into homelessness. It's the lack of affordable housing.

After moving into the shelter she began working full time at a big insurance company doing data entry to save money for an apartment. Few coworkers knew she was living in a shelter.

Nadia said, "Nobody's probably looking at me and saying, 'That woman is homeless.' And I'm willing to bet a lot of them would be surprised."

III

THE DESPERATE FIGHT FOR HOMELESS HOUSING

At dusk a homeless woman walks in the street in Venice.

"HOMES END HOMELESSNESS." THAT WAS THE SIMPLE and ultimately persuasive slogan of the Proposition HHH campaign in 2016. In November of that year, an overwhelming 77 percent of Los Angeles city voters opted to raise their own property taxes to pay for $1.2 billion in homeless housing—ten thousand units to be built over a decade. Politicians exulted in the win and vowed that after years of short-lived strategies and half-hearted measures, they would finally address the crisis with the resolve and the resources needed to bring it under control.

Never in this city has so much money been available for housing the homeless. Yet the hard part is just beginning. Despite the overwhelming support for Proposition HHH, virtually everyone involved in the process now agrees that fierce NIMBY resistance to homeless housing in some communities and the lack of political will by elected officials in the face of that resistance are the biggest potential impediments to the roll-out of housing on the scale and timeline needed to stem the increase in homelessness. There are currently more than thirty-four thousand homeless people in the city of Los Angeles.

"We did the glitzy part, but now we have to get the work done, brick by brick, block by block," says Councilman Marqueece Harris-Dawson, who represents South Los Angeles. "I predict we'll hit a wall—that we'll get stuck."

That wall could be erected by the City Council itself, whose members have nearly unfettered say over what gets built and what gets blocked in their districts—but who have been extremely reluctant over the years to challenge the fierce opposition of their most vocal constituents on the issue of homelessness. Even as the crisis has intensified, they've wavered. Councilman Jose Huizar, for instance, stalled the development for nearly two years of a well-designed, modest residential project in Boyle Heights that would have housed a mere twenty-four homeless people, partly because of objections from the business owner next door. Councilman Joe Buscaino caved to protesters in San Pedro and ditched his own perfectly reasonable plan for a storage facility where homeless people could put their belongings.

Councilman Gil Cedillo pulled a property in his district that consists of five parking lots off the list of city-owned sites suitable for homeless housing in December 2016 because, he said, the Lincoln Heights community had not been consulted; the result was a yearlong delay.

"Political will is now the biggest challenge," says former City Controller Wendy Greuel, who sits on the Los Angeles Homeless Services Authority's Board of Commissioners. "Will the City Council and the mayor and the county say, 'Yes, we will put this housing in our neighborhoods'?"

NEARLY TWO YEARS AFTER the ballot measure passed, only two projects with HHH funding have broken ground. Of eight city-owned properties identified two years ago as sites for homeless housing, not one is near construction—and these were supposed to be the easy projects, the low-hanging fruit. The city has funded 416 homeless housing units that were already in the pipeline, which is pretty good—and no one ever thought the crisis would be addressed in a single year—but new projects aren't being moved toward approval nearly quickly enough.

Until the mayor and the members of the City Council treat the building of these ten thousand units of housing with the kind of extraordinary urgency this crisis requires—the kind that the federal and state governments bestowed upon, for example, the rebuilding of the broken Santa Monica Freeway after the Northridge earthquake—they simply will not be built. And they must be built. Supportive housing in particular—which offers not just a place to live but also access to job counseling and mental health and substance abuse treatment, among other things—is the best long-term solution for the chronically homeless, whose cases are the most difficult to solve. A substantial number of these housing units must be located in every single council district. They cannot just be concentrated in poor areas or in neighborhoods with less political clout. Already, a new report shows that even more housing will be needed than was estimated at the time HHH was passed.

There will be opposition, vocal and angry. There already is. But ultimately, every council member must support a fair share of this housing in his or her district—and push back against those constituents who object by rote. We expect council members to lead rather than follow, to explain why this housing is necessary, and to push as many reasonable projects as possible through the gantlet of City Council approvals.

SURELY GARCETTI MUST BE AWARE THAT HIS MAYORALTY WILL ULTIMATELY BE JUDGED ON HOW HE HANDLES THIS CRISIS.

We expect Mayor Eric Garcetti to stand up publicly and fight for those projects as well. The mayor, who is said to be contemplating his next career steps, has an opportunity to repair the long-standing perception that he is unwilling to take on tough public battles. Surely he must be aware that his mayoralty will ultimately be judged on how he handles this crisis.

Recently, there have been signs of progress. There's talk of transforming city-owned parking lots into housing for the chronically homeless, and a separate move is underway to begin converting motel rooms to supportive housing units. There's also a proposed ordinance to speed up the time-consuming review process for approving permanent supportive housing projects, and Garcetti has joined other California mayors to request an additional $1.5 billion in state aid to address homelessness.

Members of the City Council seem to be feeling the pressure for action as well. Cedillo put the Lincoln Heights parking lots back on the city-owned property housing list in December 2017 (after his reelection and a phone call from *The Times* asking why he'd taken them off). Huizar called *The Times* just before this series was put to bed to say he'd changed his mind and would urge the City Council to approve the Boyle Heights project as soon as possible. (Huizar has backed a number of other supportive-housing projects in his district in the past.) And Buscaino has been pushing to get a homeless storage facility set up at another site in San Pedro. Those are encouraging steps.

We need to pause to say a word on behalf of Councilman Mike Bonin; more elected officials should follow his example. Few have been as courageous in fighting for homeless housing as Bonin, who has championed several controversial projects and storage facility proposals in his district, despite being unfairly savaged by some of his constituents. It's imperative that other council members be that bold and put the well-being of the city over the short-sighted fears of some constituents.

IT IS NOT SURPRISING that some city residents fear homeless housing in their neighborhoods. Roughly a third of homeless people are mentally ill. Many are substance abusers. Some seem—or are—threatening. Residents worry about security, of course, and also about what will happen to property values if homeless people move in nearby. Some believe they're being unfairly asked to bear a disproportionate share of the burden for a citywide problem. There is undoubtedly an element of prejudice—even of racism—in some people's objections to homeless housing, but others voice reasonable concerns or harbor common misconceptions about homelessness. There are plenty of legitimate land-use questions to be asked—about density, parking, height, design—although some opponents hide their fears and prejudices behind those more mundane concerns.

But the fact remains that housing must be

built and residents who live nearby must come to understand that it is better to have people housed and treated than to have them living in tent encampments on the streets. And neighbors *can* be persuaded of that. In the end, although there is often a small but vocal and implacable group of opponents, most residents are open to living near a well-designed, well-managed homeless housing development, according to providers who have seen onetime NIMBYs become supportive neighbors over time. Officials say their research shows that most people are predisposed to help the homeless, and that while they are a little apprehensive of homeless housing in their neighborhoods when they first hear about it, they can be persuaded by the right arguments, guarantees, and reassurances.

Since 2007, the city of Los Angeles has helped finance the building of 2,667 units of permanent supportive housing, according to officials.

Homeless housing is not to be imposed on communities thoughtlessly or arbitrarily. When a potential HHH project is proposed, developers must get neighbors' input—that is mandated by the city. When a West LA community was worried last year about what the affordable housing development firm Thomas Safran & Associates would build on a piece of city land that holds a now-shuttered animal shelter, the developers held at least ten meetings in the neighborhood and took people on a tour of their other low-income and homeless housing developments. Members of the firm also assured the neighborhood that the tenants—low-income seniors and homeless families—would all be background-checked. The project got the blessing of the neighborhood council.

To answer concerns about living next door to people with mental health or substance abuse problems, service providers recite their many success stories. Take, for example, the case of Emily Martiniak, sixty-five, who lived in a shelter, panhandled on the streets, and once stood on a bridge contemplating suicide. Six years ago, Martiniak moved into LA Family Housing's

Palo Verde complex. Now, she makes some money as a notary public, takes medication for her bipolar illness, and speaks to groups about homelessness.

It would be disingenuous to suggest that there are never troubling incidents in homeless housing. In the same building where Martiniak has thrived, another resident, with mental health problems that include paranoia, was deemed by service providers to need more intensive care. She was eventually evicted. Service providers absolutely should take steps to ensure that the safety concerns of neighbors are addressed. Residents of supportive housing who can't or won't abide by the rules can be removed.

In Venice, where a developer has proposed building 140 units of housing, including 68 for supportive housing, opponents have complained that their neighborhood is being saddled with more homeless housing units than other parts of the city. Every community should take its fair share, they argue.

Indeed, every community should. The City Council passed a resolution, introduced by Council President Herb Wesson, pledging to approve 222 units of homeless housing in their districts by July 2020. That's a start, but now they have to stick to it; the resolution itself is nonbinding. And more housing than that will be necessary.

Permanent supportive housing is not a quick fix. But it has the potential to be a permanent fix.

IV

HOW SOCIETY BETRAYED
THE MENTALLY ILL

Les Jones works on his computer in his studio apartment in Santa Monica.

IF ONLY WE COULD MAKE LES JONES'S STORY MORE

commonplace. As the sixty-two-year-old Texas native leans back from his desktop computer in his small apartment, he details his journey from a successful radio career to a mental breakdown, to the streets, to shelter, and finally to treatment and a healthy, happy life in this tidy complex at perhaps the most enviable corner of Santa Monica, steps from the Third Street Promenade, a short walk to the beach.

"I am one verse," Jones says of the composition of the American population of the mentally ill. "There are others. Modern treatment of mental illness produces miracles. It literally saved my life."

Jones lives at Step Up on Second, the name of the apartment building and the nonprofit organization that operates it. He is serving his second stint on Step Up's board of directors, runs a computer-training program, and helps other residents adjust to their new home.

He has lived here for eleven years.

This is permanent supportive housing. This is the type of thing Los Angeles voters are helping to build through their ballot measures and tax dollars. Jones and his neighbors each have their own apartments and lock their own doors. They visit on-site counselors and clinical staff as needed and discuss their progress, their lives, their medication. Many leave each morning for jobs.

Their lives are the promising future that policymakers and mental health professionals envisioned beginning in the 1950s, when a drug that was first developed as a sedative for surgical patients began being prescribed in psychiatric institutions and completely changed the nation's approach to mental health. It was marketed under the name Thorazine.

It was the age of medical miracles: antibiotics like penicillin, and vaccines and treatments that virtually eliminated polio, smallpox, and diphtheria. Drugs could cure almost anything. Surely they could cure mental illness.

That post-war spirit of can-do optimism contrasted with the barbaric mental health treatment of the time. In state hospitals and asylums, staff had responded to behavioral problems with tranquilizers or, in far too many cases, abuse that verged on torture. Patients were often force-fed and treated like prisoners, which in essence they were. That was to change.

The last bill that President Kennedy signed before his assassination in 1963 was the Community Mental Health Act—a landmark law to fund and build community mental health centers. The old-style state hospitals and asylums would close and patients would come home to be treated in outpatient clinics, in supportive-housing communities, or in local inpatient hospitals. In 1967, California adopted the Lanterman-Petris-Short Act, which strictly limited forced hospitalization and the involuntary medication of patients.

This was deinstitutionalization, and the

word had positive connotations. Civil libertarians supported patients recovering their self-determination. Others applauded the cost savings that came from treating people in outpatient settings. The mental health establishment—much of it anyway—expected better psychiatric outcomes and an end to abusive conditions.

SO WHAT HAPPENED? Why do so many people with mental health challenges end up on the street instead of community clinics? Why are there so few success stories like Les Jones, too few places like Step Up on Second and far too many people in Los Angeles and around the nation today who turn to street drugs like heroin instead of prescribed medication to quiet the voices in their heads, or to methamphetamine to try to ease their depression?

First, it's important to remember that the mentally ill account for only about a third of the homeless, so even if they were all properly treated and housed, homelessness would remain a monumental problem in Los Angeles.

That said, people who should be in permanent supportive housing and clinical care are on the street in large part because a society that did so well at the easy and money-saving part of deinstitutionalization—releasing the patients, laying off the staffs, closing the hospital doors—failed to follow through with the difficult and expensive part. Few of the promised clinics were built. The funding was constantly delayed. It was finally supposed to come with the Mental Health Systems Act of 1980, signed into law by President Carter. But the following year, Congress and the new president, Ronald Reagan, repealed the act.

Meanwhile, medication was not the quick and easy solution that it had been made out to be. Thorazine had serious side effects. It was replaced by a variety of other drugs, many of which do work wonders—as is the case with Jones, who says his treatment keeps his

"MODERN TREATMENT OF MENTAL ILLNESS PRODUCES MIRACLES. IT LITERALLY SAVED MY LIFE."

—LES JONES

schizo-affective disorder under control. But many patients complain they are no longer themselves when medicated.

With a dearth of clinics and supportive housing and little public appetite to pay for them, cities, counties, and states have had to scramble for their own solutions.

Many defer to nonprofit shelters, which offer meals, drug counseling, medical referrals, and job training. It's the right answer for some. Jones began his journey to recovery at such a shelter. But others battling illness or substance abuse are deterred by the strict rules of conduct or by the bans on personal belongings or pets. Bureaucratic mazes that would deter even the most emotionally fit keep mentally ill homeless people from seeking help.

Jones was lucky enough to have a place to go. If everyone on the streets could look forward to the same positive outcome, it might be easier to open more places like Step Up on Second. But many nervous would-be neighbors fear that most mentally ill homeless are unlike Jones and could never integrate safely into a community setting.

SOME MENTAL HEALTH PROFESSIONALS and elected officials believe the answer is to roll back laws that limit the ability to forcibly commit people who can't or won't seek help on their own. The LA County Board of Supervisors recently called for just such a change, presumably to deal with people whose conditions are too serious for permanent supportive housing. There are now bills in Sacramento to amend the Lanterman-Petris-Short Act's protections against compelled treatment.

In 2001, *The Times* editorial board published a series arguing that it was indeed worth sacrificing some civil liberties in order to treat people, rather than permit them to die on the street. But the issue isn't all that simple. Today, *The Times* cautiously supports reexamining existing laws on compelled treatment, as long as Californians do not mislead themselves into believing that it is an acceptable, effective, or lasting shortcut for getting a majority of people with mental health challenges off the street.

For all but the most seriously ill, the better answer is a painstaking process of trust-building. Otherwise, sick people who are run through a ponderous and liberty-depriving process will just drift back to the street. For many, successful treatment requires housing first, so that patients can drop their perpetual guard against assaults on both their personal safety and their self-determination.

Besides, forcibly committed people would still need a place to be housed and treated, and we are still without the clinics and other facilities that were supposed to come with deinstitutionalization.

By default, and to our collective shame, much of the response has been a virtual reinstitutionalization—but this time, to jail.

The largest psychiatric institutions in the

United States are the Los Angeles County jails, the Cook County Jail in Chicago, and Rikers Island in New York. LA County incarcerates thousands of mentally ill people. The Sheriff's Department reports that more than 70 percent of inmates who enter jail report a serious illness, either mental or physical. The county is moving forward with a $2-billion-plus plan to replace the aging Men's Central Jail with a new facility specifically geared toward mental health treatment—but still a jail. We're back where we started, but this time even more literally than before: Mentally ill people are prisoners.

It's not that jailers want the new business. It's a population, LA County Sheriff Jim McDonnell recently told ABC7, "that I would argue should not be treated in a jail facility."

Making jails the centerpiece of mental health treatment is a monumental betrayal not just of the mentally ill, but of the forward-looking thinkers of the 1950s and '60s who saw a path toward a more humane and civilized society.

And it is inefficient as well; treatment in jail costs more than treatment in clinics.

Los Angeles County government recently reorganized itself to recognize and respond to mental illness, addiction, criminal justice, and homelessness in an integrated fashion. Now voters have approved a housing bond and raised their sales taxes to address homelessness.

It is perhaps a thin wafer of a down payment on the long-promised funding for community mental health treatment. But the money is just the first step. Few people enthusiastically welcome permanent supportive housing to the neighborhood. Fewer still accept mental health day clinics.

So the misery on the street grows, even though, for many people, places like Step Up on Second would be a godsend.

Jones tried to explain that recently when going door-to-door to calm the fears of neighbors to a soon-to-be-built Step Up project.

More than one door was slammed in his face.

V

CAN A CITY WITH
FIFTY-EIGHT THOUSAND
HOMELESS STILL FUNCTION?

Yolanda Gutter, a mental health evaluation officer
with the LAPD, speaks with Ken Adam.

HOMELESSNESS AFFECTS THE LIVES OF ALL ANGELENOS,

not just those forced to live on the streets. And it does so almost daily, in ways large and small.

Consider the pairs of thick gloves that George Abou-Daoud has stashed inside the nine restaurants he owns on the east side of Hollywood. When a homeless person accosts his customers, Abou-Daoud says, he can no longer count on the police for help; unless there's an imminent threat to safety, he contends, they don't respond quickly and can't just haul the person away. So he's had to take matters into his own hands, literally, by physically ejecting problematic homeless people himself. That's why he has the gloves—to keep his hands clean.

Abou-Daoud's gloves are a particularly bleak symbol of the relationship between the homeless and the non-homeless. But everyone's got a story of one sort or another. Day in and day out, Metro riders step into trains with home-less people on them—often visibly disturbed or threatening, prompting nervous passengers to edge away or change cars. In downtown LA, shop owners worry that customers will opt for suburban malls to avoid the panhandlers and glassy-eyed wanderers. In Venice, besieged busi-nesses have banded together to share the cost of security guards and cleanup crews to clear gar-bage, bedding, or worse from the sidewalks.

Across the city, drivers exiting freeways routinely encounter homeless people on the off-ramps shuffling from window to window requesting money. Libraries, train stations, and public parks have become refuges for home-less people. In many residential neighborhoods and commercial districts, encampments have become a seemingly immutable fact of life.

As homelessness spreads across Los Angeles County—the official tally shows a 46 percent increase from 2013 to 2017—it is drawing two conflicting responses, at times from the same people. There's sympathy and a desire to help, but there's also a sense of being invaded and perhaps even endangered—in terms of both physical safety and public health (see, for example, the state of emergency California declared last year over a hepatitis A outbreak that spread among the homeless, or the Skirball blaze that was sparked by a cooking fire in a homeless encampment). There's an unavoidable, often unspoken, fear that the city around us may be in a state of irreversible decline, and a suspicion on the part of some that the rights of homeless people have trumped the rights of everyone else.

THE INCREASING VISIBILITY of homelessness and destitution contributes to the uneasy feeling that the problem is closing in on everyone. It's also a daily reminder that the values and systems to which we cling—liberty, democracy, free enterprise, the social contract that's supposed to hold a community together, the safety net that is supposed to protect the most vulnerable—haven't steered us out of this mess. Nor have our leaders.

It's not surprising that some Angelenos are angry or even afraid. But we need to channel those concerns into constructive action.

The city and county must find a way to balance effectively the needs and rights of homeless people against the demands and expectations of everyone else. Respecting the rights of homeless people doesn't mean consigning the sidewalks and parks permanently to tents and shopping carts, just as respecting the rights of property owners doesn't mean rousting the unsheltered and shuffling them from one neighborhood to the next. Instead, what is needed are reasonable compromises that protect the health, safety, and basic needs of homeless people while ensuring the community's ability to function day in and day out. That, in turn, requires residents and businesses not just to accept the presence of homeless people, but to have a stake in

THERE'S AN UNAVOIDABLE, OFTEN UNSPOKEN, FEAR THAT THE CITY AROUND US MAY BE IN A STATE OF IRREVERSIBLE DECLINE.

getting them off the streets and into housing. (They should start by remembering that only a minority—though a visible one—of homeless people are mentally ill or drug addicted; many are simply down on their luck and pose no threat to others.)

Some compromises have already been laid out. What's often been missing, though, is the political courage necessary to implement them. For example, the LA City Council adopted an ordinance two years ago that requires homeless people to abandon their carts and put most of their possessions in storage once the government has made a storage facility available nearby. The city, however, has been able to open only two such facilities, and only one—on Skid Row—has available storage space. Community opposition has killed or hamstrung projects in San Pedro and Venice.

Similarly, faced with mounting complaints about homeless people sleeping in their cars and campers, the council adopted an ordinance in late 2016 imposing a ban on people lodging in their vehicles overnight in residential areas. But the city has been far too slow to follow through on the safe parking areas it called for on property owned by churches, nonprofits, and public agencies. That was at the heart of the compromise, and without it, the problem is merely shifted to commercial and industrial zones. Today, there is just one small safe parking lot in the city, at a church in South Los Angeles.

Admittedly, the city and county have taken some important steps forward, and have acted with an unusual degree of coordination. For example, LA Mayor Eric Garcetti's office has been conducting weekly meetings in a "war room" of sorts to begin identifying the homeless encampments most in need of attention, and then to devote outreach workers and other resources to the people living in them in a concentrated effort to move them into housing. The encampments would then be cleared. And at Metro, teams of Los Angeles Police Department officers, outreach workers, and mental health experts now respond to calls about homeless people (which make up about half of the calls received). The point is to connect people to the services they need, rather than just hustling them off the trains and buses.

THOSE ARE THE RIGHT APPROACHES, but they're not yet making a visible difference. In Hollywood, for example, business owners say street people seem younger, more aggressive, and well aware of how limited the police response has become. As a consequence, businesses are relying more on private security guards they fund through the local business improvement district, and living with a rise in drug use and petty theft.

Sitting in one of his restaurants on Sunset Boulevard, Abou-Daoud—who says he supplies food to homeless people and has twice given them jobs—reels off a list of recent incidents. Here's one: A homeless man stretched out on that restaurant's patio floor one evening and screamed at the diners around him. "I asked him politely to leave. He gave me a blank stare," Abou-Daoud said. "What am I supposed to do?"

Some contend that the police are handicapped in their dealings with homeless people by criminal justice reform measures such as Proposition 47, which downgraded some nonviolent crimes from felonies to misdemeanors, and court orders that, for the time being, give homeless people the right to spend their nights in tents and blankets under the stars. Yet a *Times* investigation found that as the homeless population grew from 2011 to 2016, arrests of homeless people went up significantly—largely for petty crimes relating to quality-of-life issues.

If the police really backed off on arrests, there's nothing in the criminal justice reforms that compelled them to do so. Nor is it a crime to be homeless. And moving homeless people from one street or neighborhood to the next is no solution; it just moves the problem to someone else's property. Yet that's how private security officers deal with an uncooperative or problematic homeless person.

The real, durable solution is to get homeless people into housing, which means building many more apartments (the point of Proposition HHH) as well as providing the outreach workers and services needed to move people off the streets and keep them off the streets (the point of Measure H). It will take years to get those housing units built, however. Realizing they can't leave thousands of people in tents on the sidewalks in the meantime, city officials have kicked around a number of promising ways to house homeless people on a temporary basis; for example, there's a proposal to fast-track the conversion of motels into short-term rentals and a plan to put housing trailers on a city-owned lot.

The county is also preparing to send out far more outreach teams this year, eventually putting ten times as many in the field as it had before Measure H passed. And it's expanding its

211 phone service to enable callers to summon outreach teams if they need help with a homeless person.

A responsive and effective 211 service would provide at least a partial answer to Abou-Daoud's question about what Angelenos are supposed to do in the face of homelessness. But officials haven't spread the word about it yet—they're waiting until they have enough teams assembled to make the service worth calling.

At stake here is the quality of life for everyone in the county, not just the people without homes. We can't continue trying to solve the problems on the sidewalks by foisting them onto someone else. That's not striking a balance between the competing needs of the homeless and the non-homeless; it's just staying on the path that got us to this point.

VI

WHO'S TAKING CHARGE OF THE HOMELESS CRISIS?

A person sleeps at 1st and Spring Streets, across from Los Angeles City Hall.

TWO YEARS AFTER LOS ANGELES CITY LEADERS SAID THEY
were about to declare (although they never actually did) a state of emergency over a deepening homelessness crisis, and after county supervisors called on the state to declare such an emergency (it didn't); more than eighteen months after voters overwhelmingly agreed to pay $1.2 billion to house people now living on the street; a year after LA County voters raised their sales taxes by a quarter-cent on the dollar to pay for mental health care and other support services for the homeless; and now, confronting another winter in which tens of thousands of people huddled in flimsy tents or with no shelter at all will face violent Santa Ana winds, chilling nights, and seasonal downpours—where are we?

How many people have we housed, or at least, how many are we on track toward housing? Is Los Angeles setting the national standard for

HOW MANY PEOPLE HAVE
WE HOUSED, OR AT LEAST,
HOW MANY ARE WE ON
TRACK TOWARD HOUSING?

rapid and effective response to a vexing problem? Or are its leaders merely mastering the art of appearances while passing the buck and hoping things turn around?

Who knows? LA homelessness stats are spread among obscure reports from city, county, and federal agencies.

And you'll learn nothing by attending a meeting of the body charged with ending homelessness or hearing the report from the homelessness czar—the point person reporting directly to both the city's mayor and the county Board of Supervisors. That's because there is no committee and no czar with sole responsibility for ending homelessness. Or rather, there are many committees and many sub-commanders, which is almost the same as there being none at all.

WHO'S IN CHARGE HERE?

The question echoes unanswered through the streets of this notoriously fractured, siloed, and balkanized metropolis, where the city-county structure and the political culture too often allow politicians to wriggle their way out of accountability. The city of LA and eighty-seven other cities each control their own land-use policies and therefore determine what housing can be built, and where and for what purpose, while nearly every other aspect of human service for the destitute and miserable—including mental health, public health, and addiction treatment—is handled by the massive Los Angeles County government, with its five coequal supervisors and its virtually unknown chief executive.

There may be no more telling example of the poor working relationship between the city and the county—historically, anyway—than in the death of a homeless Angeleno on the street more than a quarter of a century ago. The city responded the way it knew best: by suing the county (for failing to deal with poverty). The Board of Supervisors struck back by blaming the city (for restrictive housing policies that put shelter beyond the reach of the needy). Lawyers settled the suit by creating a new entity—the Los Angeles Homeless Services Authority, better known as LAHSA—to integrate the city and county responses to homelessness. Instead of solving the problem, however, that began a decades-long battle over control of both the agency and its leadership.

Now, the county's homeless population has ballooned to nearly fifty-eight thousand. More than eight hundred homeless people died on the streets last year in Los Angeles, which puts into tragic perspective the single death that led to the creation of LAHSA in the 1990s.

The current LAHSA executive director, Peter Lynn, has not become LA's single point person on homelessness. LAHSA collects and distributes money and performs the annual homeless count in order to compile the numbers demanded by the US Department of Housing and Urban Development, but Lynn does not direct LA's homelessness operations. Lynn, LA Mayor

Eric Garcetti, and the Los Angeles County Board of Supervisors all argue that they work better together on homelessness than ever before, and that may well be true—but they move forward with their own distinct programs, policies, outreach, and messaging.

Some LA homelessness advocates look longingly toward San Bernardino County, where the Board of Supervisors contracted with former county CEO Greg Devereaux to preside over regular command sessions where department chiefs are grilled on the latest homelessness data. Where are the hot spots? Who are the newly homeless? What's blocking us from housing them? Who is responsible for removing those blocks? Why haven't you done it yet?

But San Bernardino's homelessness challenge is tiny compared with LA's. Here, a clearly frustrated City Attorney Mike Feuer is calling for a "field general" in charge of logistics for the city, evaluating the data, instilling a sense of mission, pressing council members to house a few more people in their districts, operating in a direct link with outreach workers using hand-held devices to instantly find available beds and other services with people in need—and operating as an empowered emissary of the mayor.

Yet such a czar would only be as powerful as the mayor who appointed him or her. And in LA, the mayor lacks legal authority to override City Council members, who can and do frequently say "no" to proposed housing and mental health facilities in their districts. And neither the mayor nor the czar would have control over the county, which supplies the services, or the region's other eighty-seven cities. Czar-like powers would be possible only if council members were to relinquish some land-use and budget authority through something like an emergency declaration. And remember, they never did that. They gathered together and said they were going to do it, and much of the world's media mistook that cleverly phrased promise to do it as actually doing it. You'll find news stories saying they did it. But they did not.

Meanwhile, at the county, the Board of Supervisors put experienced official Phil Ansell in charge of its Homeless Initiative. But as Ansell recently reminded the panel overseeing expenditure of Measure H sales tax money, the real roadblock to effectively dealing with homelessness—now that the money is coming in—is siting homeless housing. The county has no control over that, except in places where there is no city government, such as Marina del Rey (where land costs are prohibitive).

So now what? Do we give up?

Hardly. We instead distinguish between authority—which is granted by city charters and ordinances—and power, which is exerted by leaders with backbones and a willingness to spend their political capital when it really matters. Garcetti could, if he wanted to, call out those council members who refuse to permit construction of permanent supportive housing—or even plain-old affordable housing—in their districts. He could shame them, cajole them, buoy them, empower them, pressure them. To date, has done too little of this. In the months ahead, regardless of his plans for his political future, he needs to stay focused on solving the problems that face the city here and now.

At the same time, the city, the county, and LAHSA could demonstrate their supposedly improved collaboration by creating a single point of contact for homelessness response.

The county is retooling its 211 telephone program to direct callers to services for homeless people, and that's good. As it is now, who knows whom to call when encountering a person on the street who may be ill, or who may need a place to spend the night, or who may seem threatening? Do you call the police? The paramedics? 911?

Now, it's 211—but how many people know about it, or know whether to call that LA County number or 311, the LA city number? Whom do you call if you're in West Covina? Compton? Santa Clarita? Is it asking too much to give residents, whether comfortably housed or otherwise, a single point of contact for help with homelessness or indeed any other service regardless of municipal boundaries? We certainly do that with 911 and calls for emergency service.

The county has an online dashboard showing expenditures of Measure H funds together with outcomes—how many housed, how many served with mental health care, and the like. And that's good, but why can't we expect the same website to also inform residents of how the city's Proposition HHH housing bond funds are being spent, including how many units are being built, how many have broken ground, how many are in the pipeline? And how many units are being built in Long Beach, Burbank, and the county's other eighty-five cities? Homelessness transcends city limits. So should the solutions and the accountability measures put in place by county and city officials.

LOS ANGELES IS NOT like San Francisco or New York, where the city and county are combined in a single government. Here, cooperation and silo-busting are essential, and are not yet where they need to be. Every city and county elected official must be held to answer, individually and collectively, on a regular basis, for clearly communicating how well their programs are working, how many people they have housed—and how many they are leaving on the street.

It should go without saying that homelessness is an issue of a different magnitude than, say, fixing potholed streets or ironing out the problems in a new recycling program. This is a humanitarian tragedy of extraordinary proportions that the citizens and elected officials of this city and this county are morally obligated to solve by working together, committing resources, and, in some cases, making sacrifices.

To that end, though, the people in charge need to show that they know what to do, that they

are making tough decisions, that they are getting the most for our money, and that the problem is receding. That's what leadership requires.

ACKNOWLEDGMENTS

Many people deserve special thanks for helping make this project succeed. Once again, Steve Wasserman, the publisher and executive director at Heyday, approached us about publishing a book of our original editorials and then helped shepherd the project to completion. Thanks also to Emmerich Anklam, Mariko Conner, and Ashley Ingram at Heyday. At the *Los Angeles Times*, many people were involved in the creation, design, editing, and publication of the homelessness series, including Matthew Fleischer, Mary Cooney, Francine Orr, Albert Lee, Sean Greene, Sue Worrell, Michael Whitley, and Jim Kirk.

ABOUT THE AUTHOR

Founded in 1881, the *Los Angeles Times* is the largest news-gathering organization west of the Mississippi. Now read by more than fifty million unique visitors monthly, *The Times'* journalism has won forty-four Pulitzer Prizes, six of which were gold medals for public service.

The editorials collected in this book are the work of *The Times'* editorial board, which is responsible for determining the positions of the paper on the important issues of the day. Unlike articles written by the paper's reporters in its news pages, editorials are works of opinion. They are unsigned because they represent the consensus of the board.

The opinions expressed in these editorials were reached through a process of discussion and deliberation by editorial writers Kerry Cavanaugh, Mariel Garza, Robert Greene, Carla Hall, Karin Klein, Scott Martelle, and Michael McGough, working with editorial page editor Nicholas Goldberg and deputy editor Jon Healey.

The photographs were taken by *Los Angeles Times* staff photographer Francine Orr.

ABOUT THE PUBLISHER

Heyday is an independent, nonprofit 501(c)(3) publisher founded in 1974 in Berkeley, California. It promotes civic engagement and social justice, and celebrates California's natural beauty. Through books, public events, and outreach programs, Heyday works to give voice to the voiceless and to realize the California dream of diversity and enfranchisemcnt. In 2017, Heyday marked thirty years of publishing *News from Native California*, the state's leading magazine of Indian affairs and culture. Heyday seeks to build a vibrant community of writers and readers, activists and thinkers.

A NOTE ON TYPE

Trump Mediaeval is named after Georg Trump, its designer, who created it between 1954 and 1962. An old-style serif typeface, it was used both by the C. E. Weber foundry as metal type and Linotype for hot metal typesetting. Its classical aspect recalls earlier Venetian typefaces and is commonly associated with books of enduring merit and bespoke design. Pleasing to the eye, it is a font of balance and serenity whose proportions and aesthetic appeal are widely admired by typographic connoisseurs the world over.